T0132479

My Cat Anee
Is Up a Tree!
Lillie Land Watson
Illustrated by Shevon Wells

AuthorHouse™
1663 Liberty Drive
Bloomington, IN 47403
www.authorhouse.com
Phone: 1 (800) 839-8640

Published by AuthorHouse 03/28/2019

ISBN: 978-1-7283-0463-2 (sc)
ISBN: 978-1-7283-0464-9 (e)

Print information available on the last page.

This book is printed on acid-free paper.

authorHOUSE®

I would like to dedicate this book ***"My Cat Anee is Up a Tree"*** to my 5 beautiful children, Esteban, Davon, Bernisha, Jamila, and Lillian. All of You have and always will be my greatest inspiration of life, Love, and motivation to keep creating. You all are the greatest gift a mom could ever treasure and you continually make me proud. My heart will always beat for you, my angels. Thank you for allowing me to love you in my special way. *Love MOM!*

On a boat without a paddle!

On a horse without a saddle!

Up a tree without a ladder!

My cat Anee is up a tree!

Meow, meow is all we hear.
Anytime, that we are near,
the tree, the tree,
the tall, tall tree.
The tree that holds my cat Anee.

If my cat only knew
the only thing he has to do,
is to climb down from the tree,
and come inside and be with me.

MEOW

Father, Mother, Sister, Brother,
Do you know of any other
That will go up the tree
And get my baby cat, Anee?

MEOW

Policeman, policeman, can you see
my poor cat is up the tree?
Yes, my child, I do see
your poor cat is up the tree.
But I can’t, I wish I could.
It’s just too high, it’s too much wood.

MEOW

Fireman, fireman, can you please
Go up the tree and get my Anee?
No my child, we are not allowed.
Cause if we come, we'll draw a crowd.

MEOW

Neighbor, neighbor, you're my last

chance to my cat down fast.

Do you have a ladder please?

To get my cat down, he's

hungry and he's thirsty too.

There is nothing I won't do.

I'll walk your dog, I'll rake your yard.

My brothers they will work real hard.

They'll climb the tree and get Anee.

Do you have a ladder, please?

MEOW

Oh my child, yes I do.

I'll get my ladder just for you.

Get your brothers and I will be

waiting by that tall, tall tree.

Bird
Seed

Brothers, brothers, hurry, hurry.

We no longer have to worry.

Our neighbor did agree

to help you get my cat Anee.

He'll bring a ladder big and tall.

One's that strong, you will not fall.

Anee was glad and so was I.
To see their faces and say goodbye
to that tree, that tall, tall tree,
the tree that held my cat Anee.

Now he's home. He's warm and fed.

With me he's lying in my big soft bed.

Everyone around here knows, that my two brothers are my heroes!

My
HEROES

About Anee my Cat

Ever since I could remember, I have always enjoyed having cats and dogs in my life. I really just love animals. All animals in fact. They have their way of interacting with you just as a person, if you pay attention to them. Just as we are, animals have stories to tell as well. We found Anee at the animal shelter when he was about 4 months. The first thing he did was got stuck up our tree in the front of our house. We never figured out how he got up there so high. So all of these books are based on true stories about our cat Anee. He has always gotten into trouble. He would run my daughters through the house if he would get upset with them or he didn't get his way. He loved to catch other animals. As my daughter was taking a bath he was curious as to what water was and he accidentally jumped into the tub with my daughter. Rub a dub a dub story. And when a doctor came to see my sick son, Anee was on top of his vehicle and he was riding on top of the doctor's car and then I wrote the book. Have you heard the news, Anee's taking a car cruise. Anee would always find something mischief to get into. There are more stories about Anee. He died at the age of 14. We really missed him but he left a lot of stories to be told by me. I am going to tell them in the books I write as best as I can.

My name is **Lillie Land Watson**. I was married 35 years and I am the mother of 5 wonderful children. I am an artist and I love to play my guitar and write songs. I enjoy doing photography and I love to write stories. As I would drive or sometimes when I am alone, I always think about the what if's with life and things I may see as I am driving. So I've decided to write about them, my thoughts that is. So with this, I know how much I love to write. When I was in high school, one of my favorite books to read was Nancy Drew Mysteries. I even wrote a mystery book of my own at a young age. I have driven my children back and forth to school for 15 years so I can be with them. I have enjoyed listening to many of the children stories, of their adventures with friends and adventures in school.. I will continue writing stories about Anee, and hopefully he will make my readers as happy as he did for me and my family.

Printed in the United States
By Bookmasters